O9-AIF-092

Christmas Puzzles
Puzzle Mania

HIGHLIGHTS PRESS
Honesdale, Pennsylvania

Contents

When you finish a puzzle, check it off √.
Good luck, and happy puzzling!

Arts & Crafts

A-Mazing!

Fun & Games

Hidden Pictures

Wordplay

Holiday Wrap-Up

All of these letters were hung with care in hopes that some puzzlers soon would be here. These holiday words are all hidden in this grid. Search up, down, across, diagonally, and backward to find them.

Word list:
- CELEBRATION
- CANDLES
- CHRISTMAS
- DANCE
- DREIDEL
- FIRST CROPS
- GIFTS
- HANUKKAH
- HARVEST
- JOY
- KARAMU
- KINARA
- KISLEV
- KWANZAA
- MENORAH
- MISTLETOE
- SHAMMASH
- STOCKING
- TINSEL
- TREE

Grid:

```
U M I S T L E T O E D A
N M H A N U K K A H J S
S H A M M A S H X A S P
V H R R N Q Y D S A T O
O A V V A O T A W Z O R
S R E E J K M N S N C C
E O S L R T L C E A K T
L N T S L L C E D W I S
D E K I N A R A S K N R
N M R K S T F I G N G I
A H D R E I D E L R I F
C E L E B R A T I O N T
```

Art by Jeff Shelly

Hidden Pictures
Making Cookies

Can you find the **17** objects hidden in the big picture?

magnifying glass

question mark

crescent moon

wedge of cheese

book

comb

oar

drum

crown

flag

leaf

tube of toothpaste

test tube

spool of thread

top hat

shuttlecock

seashell

Reindeer Games

Can you help Herbie find which reindeer
or pair of reindeer is tied to each lead?

1 2 3 4 5

Art by Jeff Shelly

What's Wrong?

How many silly things can you find in this picture?

Art by Chuck Dillon

9

Follow the Flakes

Can you find a path from **START** to **FINISH** that adds up to **21**? You can move across, up, down, or diagonally from one snowflake to the next.

START

FINISH

On the Tree

Branch out! Adorn the holiday evergreen with ornaments made by you.

Yarn Wreath

1. Thread **beads** on a length of **yarn**.

2. Loosely wrap the yarn around your hand about twenty times to form a circle.

3. Cut eight pieces of yarn, each about 6 inches long. Tie each piece, evenly spaced, around the wreath. Knot and trim the yarn ends.

4. Decorate the wreath with a yarn bow.

5. To hang, make a loop from another piece of yarn and tie in the back.

Sled Ornament

1. Line up five **craft sticks** in a sled shape.

2. Spread glue along another stick. Place it across the other sticks, about 1 inch from the top of the center stick. Let dry.

3. Decorate the sled as you like.

4. To hang, glue a **ribbon** or **yarn** loop to the back.

Rudolph Ornament

1. Glue two **craft sticks** together to form a narrow V shape.

2. Glue a third stick about an inch down from the top of the V. Let dry.

3. Add a **red paper** nose, **plastic wiggly eyes**, and **paper** holly leaves and berries.

4. To hang, glue **ribbon** or **yarn** to the back of Rudolph's ears.

Cookie Code

We listed **10** kinds of cookies here. It's up to you to crack the code and fill in the names. Each number stands for a different letter. Once you know one number's letter, you can fill in that letter in all of the words. Grab some milk and get started!

1. M A C A R O O N
   7 10 1 10 11 2 2 8

2. L E M O N B A R
   6 5 7 2 8 9 10 11

3. S U G A R
   13 18 12 10 11

4. F O R T U N E
   19 2 11 16 18 8 5

5. G I N G E R S N A P
   12 4 8 12 5 11 13 8 10 14

6. S H O R T B R E A D
   13 15 2 11 16 9 11 5 10 17

7. O A T M E A L R A I S I N
   2 10 16 7 5 10 6 11 10 4 13 4 8

8. P E A N U T B U T T E R
   14 5 10 8 18 16 9 18 16 16 5 11

9. C H O C O L A T E C H I P
   1 15 2 1 2 6 10 16 5 1 15 4 14

10. S N I C K E R D O O D L E
    13 8 4 1 3 5 11 17 2 2 17 6 5

Bonus Puzzle

Did you fill in all the names? Use the same code to answer this riddle.

What did the gingerbread man use to trim his fingernails?

A C O O K I E C U T T E R
10 1 2 2 3 4 5 1 18 16 16 5 11

Hidden Pictures
A New Friend

Can you find the **14** objects hidden in the big picture?

bird

bowl

ship

candle

flag

dinosaur

crescent
moon

ladder

ice-cream
cone

beet

top hat

ring

game
piece

sock

13

Downhill Run

Whee! Bianca is about to head down the slope.
Can you help her ski safely to the bottom?

Start

or

Finish

Art by Mike Moran

Hidden Pictures

Welcome to the North Pole

Can you find the **12** objects hidden in the big picture?

Art by R. Michael Palan

ring

balloon

crescent moon

shoe

light bulb

toothbrush

lollipop

golf club

muffin

fish

drinking straw

candle

Art by Dave Joly

Crafts

Gift-Wrap Stampers

By Makiko Orser

1. Cut a 1-inch-by-5-inch strip from **thin cardboard**.
2. In the center of the strip, draw a design with **fabric paint**, keeping the paint at an even height. Let it dry.
3. With the design facing outward, fold back the strip above and below the design. **Staple** the ends together to form a handle.
4. Holding the stamper by the handle, press the design onto an **ink pad**. Then stamp the design onto a large sheet of **paper**, pressing down firmly and evenly so the design prints clearly. Keep stamping, using different colors and stamps if you wish, until you've decorated the whole sheet of paper. Use the paper to wrap a gift.

Christmas

Hanukkah

Kwanzaa

Dapper Penguin Ornament

By Chris Johnson

1. Cut out a head-and-body shape and two wings from black **craft foam**. Glue the wings to the body. Cut out a face and a stomach from white craft foam, and glue them on.
2. Thread a **large-eye needle** with **string**. Poke the needle through the top of the penguin's head and tie the string to form a hanger.
3. Cut out a beak, a hat, a bow tie, and feet from craft foam. Glue them on. Add **wiggle eyes** and **buttons**.

Cards for Christmas and Hanukkah

By April Theis

MERRY CHRISTMAS!

Inside the Card

HAPPY HANUKKAH!

1. Fold a piece of **cardstock** in half.
2. On the front of the card, cut off the two bottom corners to make a triangle flap.
3. For the Hanukkah card, trace around the triangle flap onto another piece of cardstock. Cut out the triangle, and glue it onto the flap to make a Star of David. Decorate it with **glitter glue** and **colored paper**. Write "Happy Hanukkah!"
4. For the Christmas card, write "Merry Christmas!" Then open the flap and use paper and glue to create a Nativity scene.

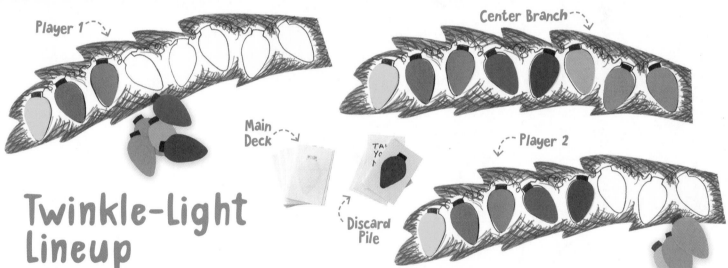

Player 1

Center Branch

Main Deck

Discard Pile

Player 2

Twinkle-Light Lineup
A Game for 2 Players

By Edna Harrington

1. Cut out a light bulb from **poster board**. Use it as a template to draw a row of eight bulbs on poster board. Draw a branch around the row, and cut it out. Make two more branches. Use **markers** to color the edges green.

2. Use the bulb template to cut out three bulbs from eight colors of **paper**.

3. Cut out 34 cards from poster board. Draw light bulbs on 32 of them. Color the bulbs (or glue on paper ones) to match the bulb colors from step 2. Make four cards of each color. Write "Take your next color" on the remaining two cards.

To Play: Give each player a branch and 8 light bulbs (one of each color). Place another branch in the center, with 8 light bulbs on it. Players will fill their own branches, from left to right, with bulbs in the same color order as the center branch. Shuffle the cards, and place the stack facedown. Take turns drawing cards, and place a bulb on your branch only if the card shows the next color you need. Discard after each turn. If you draw "Take your next color," place the next color you need on the branch. Reshuffle and use the discard pile as needed. The first player to fill his or her string of lights wins.

Break the

Beware of icy conditions ahead. Circle the **30** words containing ICE hidden in this grid. The word ICE has been replaced with 🧊. Look up, down, across, backward, and diagonally. The uncircled letters answer the snowy trivia question. We did one to get you started.

Word List

ADVICE	NICEST
BICEPS	NOTICE
CHOICES	OFFICER
COWARDICE	OVERPRICED
CREVICE	POLICE
DEVICE	PRACTICE
ICEBERG	REJOICE
ICEBOX	SACRIFICE
ICED TEA	SERVICE
ICEMAKER	SLICED
JUICES	SOLSTICE
JUSTICE	~~SPICE~~
LICENSE	TRICERATOPS
LICORICE	TWICE
MALICE	VOICEMAIL

TRIVIA QUESTION:

If one inch of rain fell as snow instead, how much snow would you have, on average? Put the uncircled letters in order on the blanks.

ANSWER:

____ _____ _____ ____

_____ __ _____.

Ice

Hidden Pictures
A Puzzling Present

Michiko knows her grandmother loves jigsaw puzzles. So she asked her grandfather to help her shop for the perfect gift for Grandma. But other puzzling objects appear on the shelves and around the store. Can you find the **8** objects hidden in the big picture?

candy cane

bottle

carrot

envelope

wedge of cheese

sugar bowl

soda can

screwdriver

Holiday Countdown
Also try to spy:

- 8 red checkers
- 4 string puzzles
- 3 green blocks
- 3 pink balls
- 3 stools
- 2 puzzle cubes
- 1 red box

Art by Paula Pertile; Photos © Thinkstock (presents) and iStockphoto.com/Okea (background)

Scrambled Scarves

Matt, Katie, David, and Grace chose a windy day for sledding. Their scarves have blown away! Use the clues to figure out whose scarf is whose. Then find **4** paths in the snow that will lead each friend to the correct scarf.

Clues

Katie's scarf does not have a fringe. Matt's scarf has more than two colors. David's scarf is next to Matt's scarf. Grace's scarf matches her coat.

Matt

Katie

David

Grace

1

2

3

4

Art by David Helton

Precise Ice

Recreate this image without crossing over any lines or removing your pencil from the page.

Art by Barbara Gray

Knit Pick

Follow each person's yarn to see what he or she is knitting.

Art by Jim Paillot

Hidden Pictures
Good Enough to Eat!

Can you find the **17** objects hidden in the big picture?

grapes

ruler

golf club

saltshaker

comb

mug

toothbrush

ice-cream cone

boot

doughnut

telescope

lollipop

envelope

cupcake

magic wand

slice of pie

hockey stick

Art by Neil Numberman

27

Double Snowmen

There are **16** differences between these pictures. How many can you find?

Santa's Coming to Town

Santa is bringing presents to the Harris kids. Use the clues below to help Santa figure out who gets which gift.

Use the chart to keep track of your answers. Put an **X** in each box that can't be true and an **O** in boxes that match.

	Video Game	Skateboard	Basketball	Puzzle	Books
Mike					
Dave					
Christy					
Neal					
Jessica					

1. Mike and Neal like to play outside.
2. Jessica's gift has multiple pieces.
3. Neal's present does not bounce.
4. Christy's present does not have pages.

Match-Up↑ BRRRR!

Each of these hats has an exact match—except for **1** hat that has no twin. Can you find it?

Getting Ready for

Casey helped a boy pick up books that he dropped.

Advent Tree

Count down to Christmas with a good deed every day.

1. Cut out a tree from **colored paper**. Glue it onto **poster board**.

2. Glue or tape a **dowel** to the top edge of the poster board. Add a **yarn** hanger.

3. With friends or family, make 24 ornaments. Glue a piece of **white paper** to the back of each one. Place the ornaments in a basket near the tree.

4. Each day, starting on December 1, take turns writing a good deed that you did that day on the back of an ornament. Add it to the tree.

5. On December 25, add a paper star to the top of the tree, which now will be covered with ornaments!

What Is Advent?

The word Advent means "arrival" or "coming." For many Christians, Advent is the season to celebrate the coming of Jesus Christ, whom Christians believe to be the Messiah. The season begins four Sundays before Christmas Day and leads up to Christmas, when many Christians celebrate Jesus's birth. People sometimes use Advent calendars (often starting on December 1) as a fun way to prepare their minds and hearts for Christmas.

Christmas?

Enjoy these crafts with your family.

Away in a Manger

Create your own Nativity scene! Use the materials below, or come up with your own ideas.

pompom

fuzzy stick

craft foam

paper baking cup

square tissue box

colored paper

cotton balls

craft stick

clothespins

yarn

clothespins

felt-covered Styrofoam ball

yarn

pompom

fabric

fabric-covered cardboard tube

thin cardboard

Winter Find

The names of **16** wintry things are hidden in the letters. Some words are across. Others are up and down. We found COCOA. Can you find the rest?

Word list

BLIZZARD
BOOTS
~~COCOA~~
ICE
ICICLES
MITTENS
PARKA
SCARF
SLED
SLEET
SKATE
SKIS
SNOWBALL
SNOWFLAKE
SNOWMAN
SNOWSHOE

```
S N O W F L A K E I
N G M I T T E N S C
O B O O T S J Q N I
W L V S K I S X O C
S I Y N J V C Y W L
H Z C O C O A S B E
O Z G W P A R K A S
E A J M Q V F A L L
Q R V A I C E T L E
Y D G N S L E E T D
```

Snow Pal

Draw something you can make with snow.

Hidden Pictures
The Perfect Tree

Can you find the **20** objects hidden in the big picture?

peanut

chef's hat

turtle

crescent moon

dolphin

envelope

seashell

spool of thread

flashlight

yo-yo

chili pepper

horseshoe

ghost

heart

broccoli

book

candy cane

game piece

chocolate chip

fish

37

Christmas Crossword

This puzzle features questions about many of the songs and stories of the Christmas holiday.

ACROSS

1. "It came upon a _____ clear"
7. "_____ beginning to look a lot like Christmas"
9. Percussion instrument played by little boy
10. Number of times Santa will check his list
12. Miser from *A Christmas Carol*
13. Santa's entrance to a house
16. "I tossed back the shutter and threw up the _____"
18. "They used to laugh and call him _____"
20. Kisses are exchanged beneath this plant.
21. Three of them were from the Orient.
23. Material of which the little soldier was made
25. Hot drink for winter
27. Reindeer who became famous one foggy eve
28. Santa's helpers
29. People put presents under this.

DOWN

1. Not even this creature was stirring.
2. Christmas ballet
3. He stole Christmas.
4. Put a ribbon in place
5. Prancer's partner
6. Another name for Santa Claus
8. Snowflake dressed in a gown
9. Hang a wreath here.
11. Famous dancing snowman
14. Places for travelers to stay
15. The night before Christmas
17. Santa's workshop is at the North _____ .
19. Father's partner
22. You could even say Rudolph's nose does this.
24. Number of reindeer on Santa's team
25. Tiny character of Dickens book
26. Song title: "_____ Maria"

Wrapping Up

Amber, Billy, Chad, and Daphne each gave their friend Eli a holiday present. But they forgot to put tags on the gifts. Using the clues below, can you figure out which friend gave Eli which gift?

Use the chart to keep track of your answers. Put an **X** in each box that can't be true and an **O** in boxes that match.

	Red Gift	Blue Gift	Yellow Gift	Green Gift	Red Bow	Blue Bow	Yellow Bow	Green Bow
Amber								
Billy								
Chad								
Daphne								

1. No gift has the same color wrapping paper and bow.
2. A girl gave a yellow gift with a red bow.
3. Billy did not put a green bow on his gift.
4. Amber did not give a red gift, nor did it have a red bow.
5. Billy used his favorite color, blue, to wrap his gift.

Puzzle by Cynthia Elam; Photo © 2010 Thinkstock

Precise Ice

Recreate this image without crossing over any lines or removing your pencil from the page.

Crafts

Sweets Prince

1. Glue **construction-paper** decorations on an empty **46-ounce beverage can** or **oatmeal container**.

2. Trace the bottom of the container on cardboard. Draw feet out from the circle, and cut out the shape. **Paint** it black. Let dry. Glue the feet to the can.

3. For the hat, ask an adult to cut the bottom from a **2-liter beverage bottle**. Paint it black. Let dry. Tape on a **yarn** hat strap.

4. Fill the can with **treats**. Place the hat on top. If needed, crumple **paper** inside the hat so it doesn't slide down.

Choir of Angels

1. For each angel, curve a half of a **paper plate** into a cone. Staple, glue, or tape in place.

2. Cut wings from the rim of another plate. Decorate the body and wings with **paint** and **glitter**.

3. Cut a face, hands, and songbook from **paper**. Glue them and the wings to the body.

4. Twist a **fuzzy stick** into a halo and tape behind the angel's head.

Reindeer Garland

fold   fold

1. Cut a 16-inch-by-3-inch strip of **construction paper**. Fold it in half three times.

2. With the folds at the sides, draw a reindeer head. The nose and antler tips should lie on the folded edges, as shown.

3. With paper still folded, cut out the reindeer, leaving shapes attached at the nose and antlers.

4. Open the chain. Draw and color the noses and eyes.

Tic Tac Row

Each of these snow globes has something in common with the other 2 snow globes in the same row. For example, in the first row across, all 3 snow globes have ice rinks inside. Look at the other rows across, down, and diagonally. Can you tell what's alike in each row?

Art by Garry Colby

Hidden Pictures
Santa's Day Off

Can you find the **14** objects hidden in the big picture?

Art by Neil Numberman

bell

banana

magnifying glass

saw

mallet

mitten

fishhook

dog bone

snake

frying pan

pencil

ruler

spoon

toothbrush

Let It Snow

There's *snow* much to do!
Get busy and **COLOR** each
hidden object that you find.
Can you find all **15**?

Art by David Helton

Christmas-Tree Farm

While everyone is looking for the perfect Christmas tree, solve this riddle! Read each clue to find out which letters to put in each numbered space, then spell out the answer below.

1. This letter is on an orange shirt.
2. This letter is on the roof.
3. This letter is on something yellow.
4. Look for this letter on top of a car.
5. A father and son carry this letter.
6. This letter is in the snow.
7. This letter is being chopped down.
8. Look for this letter by the saplings.
9. Look for this letter on a blue jacket.
10. This letter is by the cash register.
11. Look for this letter on a group of seven trees.
12. A tree is going through this letter.
13. Look for this letter by a baby.
14. This letter is in the middle of a tree.

WHY ARE CHRISTMAS TREES SUCH BAD KNITTERS?

$\overline{\ }_{2}\ \overline{\ }_{10}\ \overline{\ }_{12}\ \overline{\ }_{8}\quad \overline{\ }_{4}\ \overline{\ }_{5}\ \overline{\ }_{7}\ \overline{\ }_{4}\ \overline{\ }_{8}\ \overline{\ }_{1}\quad \overline{\ }_{3}\ \overline{\ }_{9}\ \overline{\ }_{13}\ \overline{\ }_{11}$

$\overline{\ }_{2}\ \overline{\ }_{10}\ \overline{\ }_{12}\ \overline{\ }_{14}\ \overline{\ }_{9}\quad \overline{\ }_{6}\ \overline{\ }_{12}\ \overline{\ }_{12}\ \overline{\ }_{3}\ \overline{\ }_{5}\ \overline{\ }_{12}\ \overline{\ }_{1}.$

Art by David Coulson

Snowshoe Globes

There are **16** differences between these snow globes. How many can you find?

Art by Kevin Zimmer

Double Skis

There are **12** differences between these pictures. How many can you find?

49

'Tis the Season

Fun Things to Do

1. Tie a bow around the rim of potted household plants.

2. Organize a sing-along, using homemade instruments.

3. Dress up a window with tissue-paper snowflakes.

4. Create festive place mats with stickers, markers, and cut paper. Cover with clear self-adhesive paper.

5. With an adult's permission, record a holiday greeting on your telephone answering machine.

Yum!

OPEN

Best Wishes

Send your merriest messages in a special greeting card.

Ready-to-Mail Card

1. Fold a sheet of **construction paper** into thirds. Cut 3 inches from the width. The folded paper should now measure about 6 inches by 4 inches.

2. Trim the top third to look like an envelope flap.

3. Glue a piece of light-colored **paper** inside. Glue cut-paper decorations around it. Cut out a "seal," and glue the top of it to the flap.

4. On the light-colored paper, write a message to a relative or friend. Glue the seal to close the envelope.

5. Address the front, put a stamp on it, and mail!

Felt Card

1. Fold a piece of white **poster board** to form a card. Cut it to fit your envelope if you will be mailing the finished card. Cut and glue a piece of colored **construction paper** on the front of the card.

2. Cut **felt** shapes and glue to the front of the card.

3. Add paper details if you wish. Write a greeting inside.

Art by Judith Moffatt

Winter Word Mash

Can you figure out these snowy word combos?
We did the first one for you.

1. ❄ + 🏐 = ⚪
2. ❄ + 👞 = ?
3. ❄ + 🌍 = ?
4. ❄ + 🔶 = ?
5. ❄ + 🧑 = ?
6. ❄ + 🎐 = ?

52

Art by Kevin Zimmer

Go for a Spin

Use the clues below to fill in the boxes of this spiral—**but there's a twist:** The last letter of each word is also the first letter of the next word. Use the linking letters to help you spin all the way to the center. We did the first one for you.

1. Activity in which you slide down a snowy hill

8. These keep your hands warm.

13. An ice crystal that falls from the sky in winter

21. Santa's helpers

25. Wrap this around your neck to stay warm.

29. Water _____ at 32° Fahrenheit.

35. What you get when snow and ice start to melt

39. Warm chocolaty drink (2 words)

46. Where you find the South Pole

55. Where you find the North Pole

60. Heavy outer article of clothing

63. These may chatter when you're cold.

67. Warms

71. You can build this "guy" outside after a winter storm.

77. Cold toes sometimes feel this way.

80. What winds do

83. Coldest season of the year

88. Where you ice-skate or play hockey

91. Makes hats out of wool

95. Season that marks the end of cold weather

1 S L E D D I N G
35 39
63 67
8
88
60 83
29
71
91
80 46
95 13
25 55
77
21

Snow Code

Using this snowflake alphabet, see if you can figure out what the skaters are saying.

Hidden Pictures
Christmas in the City

Can you find the **14** objects hidden in the big picture?

skateboard

golf club

slice of cake

comb

hammer

eyeglasses

flashlight

paintbrush

paper airplane

ice-cream cone

harmonica

tack

toothbrush

cupcake

Art by Neil Numberman

Warm Homecoming

A big cup of hot chocolate is waiting for this skier at the end of the trail. Can you find the path that will lead to it?

Start

Finish

Art by Barbara Gray

Festive Word Hunt

It's beginning to look a lot like Christmas! Can you find **17** words that make the holidays special in the word search below by looking up, down, backward, and diagonally?

Word list

BOW
CANDY CANE
CARD
CHIMNEY
DECORATIONS
ELVES
FAMILY
GIFT
LIGHTS

ORNAMENTS
PRESENTS
REINDEER
SANTA CLAUS
SLED
STOCKINGS
TINSEL
TOYS

```
L I G H T S M H E D D S U W Z
S T O C K I N G S I T H D G S
J W V S L E D B W N C D T P M
H M L G T I N S E L R F W R T
G Q R C O B D M A A I I C E O
E L V E S I A M C G V P N S Y
F J X G I N K L O W U E D E S
G A N O R N C A N D Y C A N E
N Q M O X C D F Q I Z M F T N
K G G I M K L E W G T E D S J
N M S L L Q W G E A P E W A V
I F I P B Y M D Z R K A M V J
K O O U O V C H I M N E Y Y Z
G V U U W S A N T A C L A U S
D E C O R A T I O N S L Y N K
```

Art by Nina Mata

Hidden Pictures
Santa's Workshop

Can you find the **16** objects hidden in the big picture?

egg

pennant

open book

bird

domino

ring

raindrop

needle

oar

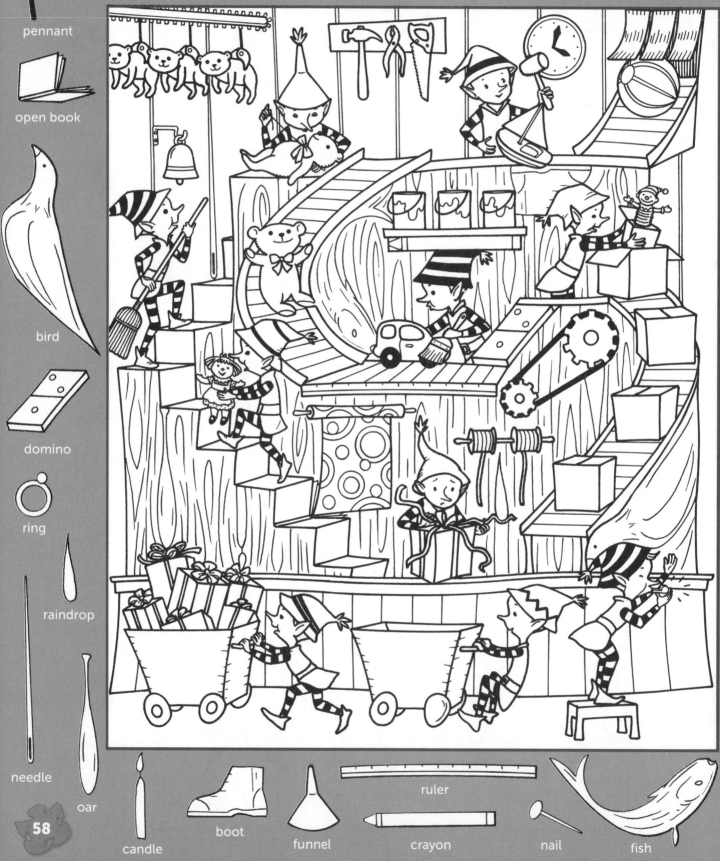

candle

boot

funnel

ruler

crayon

nail

fish

Art by Gary Mohrman

58

Tricky Trees

Each of these trees has the numbers **1** through **6** running along the sides. And in each triangle, each side adds up to the number in the middle. Can you place the numbers in each triangle so that everything adds up correctly? Each of the numbers 1 through 6 is only used once in a triangle.

Photo by iStockphoto.com/jag_cz

FLAKE SEARCH

Art by Scott Burroughs

61

Winter Word Hunt

It sure is a frosty day! Find **20** words in the snowman word search, and then look for these **7** wintry hidden objects: **boot, coat, knitted cap, shovel, skate, sled, snowplow.**

```
        T   J V E
        E   A C H E
        E   I H Z F
    X   L   Q D E R V
        S   L O J O
        R   H J A S
        A   T M B T
        K   M L E V
    S   N   O W B K E     L
    S   I   W S T A E     F
        Z   S T E R O     F
        X   T T V R Q
        A   C I F R I
    C   N   I O W I R     F
    W   O   N S T T E     F
        D   B O S L D
        P   O O E D
        L   T W
        O
        W
```

BOOT   FIRE   HAT   SKATE   SNOW

COAT   FLAKE   ICE   SKIS   SNOWBALL

COLD   FORT   PLOW   SLED   WIND

DRIFT   FROST   SHOVEL   SLEET   WINTER

Hidden Pictures
Christmas Party Fun

Can you find the **15** objects hidden in the big picture?

Art by Mark Corcoran

fish

wrench

drum

elephant

olive   pencil

traffic light

kite

baby's rattle

dinosaur

shuttlecock

baseball bat

flashlight

game piece

crown

63

Snow Angels

The Simmons sisters wound up in a tangle while playing in the snow. Can you tell which sister is wearing which scarf?

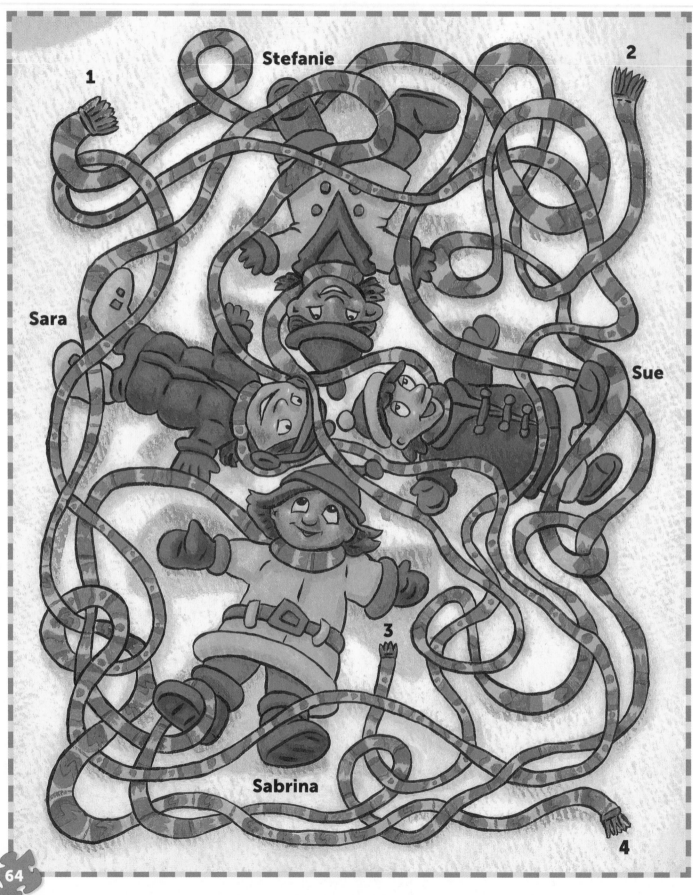

Art by T. F. Cook

Snowflake Path

This nuthatch sees a path between the snowflakes to the seeds below. Do you?

Y O U H A T S D P S O O Y D I R I T

String together the letters on the correct path to find a message.

Art by Sherry Neidigh

Crafts

Reindeer Treat Bag

By Janet Kent

1. Fold down the top third of a **brown paper bag**.

2. Decorate the bag with a **pompom** nose, **wiggle eyes**, and **markers**.

3. Use **cardstock** to make antlers and a bow. Glue or tape them on.

4. Fill the bag with treats and give it as a gift.

Snow Bank

By A.K. Pilenza

1. Cover a **cardboard box** with white **cardstock**.

2. Cut out a nose, mouth, eyes, earmuff strip, and other details from cardstock. Glue them on.

3. Ask an adult to cut a slit in the top of the box (to insert money) and a flap in the back (to remove money).

4. For earmuffs, cover two **applesauce cups** with **felt**. Glue them over the ends of the earmuff strip.

Menorah Place Card

By April Theis

1. Cover a small **cardboard tube** with **craft foam**. Cut two slits opposite each other on one end of the tube.

2. Cut a half circle and a row of nine candles from craft foam. Glue **thin cardboard** to the back of the half circle.

3. Color in the candle flames with **markers**. Glue the candles to the back of the thin cardboard. Insert the half circle into the tube's slits.

4. Make a place card for each person in your family. Use **paint** or markers to write "Happy Hanukkah!" and a name on each place card.

HAPPY HANUKKAH!

Lily

Craft samples by Buff McAllister. Photos by Hank Schneider, except page 67 (top) by Guy Cali Associates, Inc.

Countdown to New Year's!
A Game for Two Players

By April Theis

1. Cut two triangles from **poster board**.

2. Cut 20 small circles and 2 large circles from **cardstock**.

3. Glue 10 small circles to each triangle. Use **markers** to write a number on each and connect them, as shown.

4. Write "Happy New Year!" on the large circles. Glue them to the top of the triangles. Decorate them like party hats.

5. For the spinner, cut an arrow from cardstock. Punch a hole in it. Cover the inside of a **plastic lid** with cardstock. Write "Move back one" on one quarter of the spinner. Write "Move ahead one" on the rest of the spinner. Attach the arrow to the center of the lid using a **metal fastener**.

To Play: Each player places a **pompom** on number 10 on a party hat and takes turns spinning and following the instructions. Whoever reaches the large circle first wins!

Jingle-Bell Ornaments

By Linda Bloomgren

1. Twist one end of a **fuzzy stick** into a loop. Twist a **jingle bell** onto the other end.

2. Use **colored paper** and **stickers** to create a Nativity scene, a Christmas tree, or a bell. Tape the fuzzy stick to the back. Add a **yarn** bow.

67

Winter Wonder

Somewhere on these slopes are **3** sets of twins.
Can you find them?

Art by Bill Basso

Hidden Pictures
Mele Kalikimaka!

Can you find the **12** objects hidden in the big picture?

hourglass

ballet slipper

Christmas bulb

crayon

pinecone

snowflake

boot

glove

pea pod

sailboat

feather

rabbit

Art by Jennifer Zivoin

Snowman Match

Can you find the **2** snowmen that are the same?

Let's Skate!

Can you find your way to the finish line? Start at the **6** in the top corner. You may move to a new box by adding **4** or subtracting **3**. Move up, down, left, or right.

6	10	14	1
7	7	11	6
11	4	8	1

8

14

21

25

13

17

15

2

16

13

11

FiNish

Art by Kevin Zimmer

Precise Ice

A champion will be able to make this shape without crossing over or going back along any lines.

Art by Barbara Gray

74

That's a Wrap!

Purrcy, Mittens, and Lucy are wrapping presents for their feline friends. Can you find what they need in the word search below? To find the items, look up, down, across, and diagonally.

Word list

BAG	GIFT	TAPE
BOW	PRESENT	TISSUE PAPER
BOX	RIBBON	WRAPPING PAPER
CARD	SCISSORS	

```
D Z H C T O Y Z Q T G F B
J I M A A C P B B T I F N
U X M R P H L A G E F U Z
T Q Y D E V Q B O H T Z G
S C I S S O R S D F K M A
Y T I S S U E P A P E R U
M A H V D P G R R P I Y H
M S J S P A N E T G V B T
R I B B O N R S Q W E O B
H P M M B K G E A Z Q X O
Y T Z Z G A O N G Q X I W
X P K K K B X F T U H Y Z D
W R A P P I N G P A P E R
```

House Sweet House

Do you want to help judge the local gingerbread house-decorating competition? All the gingerbread houses have a twin—except 1. Find the house that doesn't have a match.

The Cold and the Beautiful

Chill with these snowflake facts, and then **COLOR** each hidden object that you find. Can you find all **13**?

Snowflakes are created when cold air turns the water vapor inside a cloud into ice crystals. The ice crystals get bigger and turn into snowflakes.

Snowflakes aren't frozen raindrops. Frozen rain is sleet.

No two snowflakes are alike because no two snowflakes experience the exact same temperature, humidity, and wind currents when they're being formed.

A snowflake's size and shape are determined by the temperature and humidity inside a cloud.

Each snowflake takes 15 to 45 minutes to form and fall to the ground.

Snowflakes look very different, but they all generally have six sides.

Puzzle by Carmen Morais; Art by David Helton

Snow Go!

You won't be snow "bored" if you find the clear path to the FINISH flag. If you run into a black line, you're going the wrong way!

START

FINISH

Art by R. Michael Palan

80

Crafts

Holiday Napkin Rings

1. Cut 1-inch- or 2-inch-wide sections from a **cardboard tube**.

2. Decorate the rings as you like. You can use **yarn**, **ribbon**, or **gift wrap paper** cutouts or a **tag** with each guest's name.

Pinecone Centerpiece

1. Glue a small **wooden candleholder** to the center of an old CD.

2. Glue **pinecones** around the candleholder.

3. Brush glue over the pinecones and sprinkle with **glitter**.

4. Place a **candle** in the candleholder.

Napkin Caddy

1. On each side of a **clear plastic detergent bottle**, draw the shape shown at right, starting an inch up from the bottom. Cut along the line. Discard the top and sides.

2. Cut and glue **felt** to cover the bottle. Add **lace** or **ribbon** at the bottom.

3. Glue on a felt design. Add **beads**, **sequins**, or other decorations.

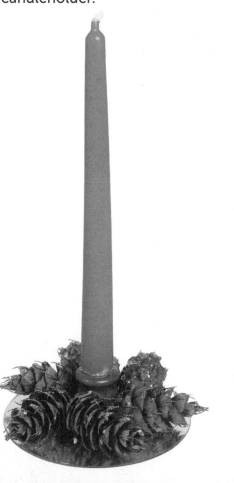

Photo © iStockphoto.com/Earnest Tse

81

Mitten Search

Can you find **10** mittens on the next page?
Color in a mitten in this box each time you find a mitten in the picture.

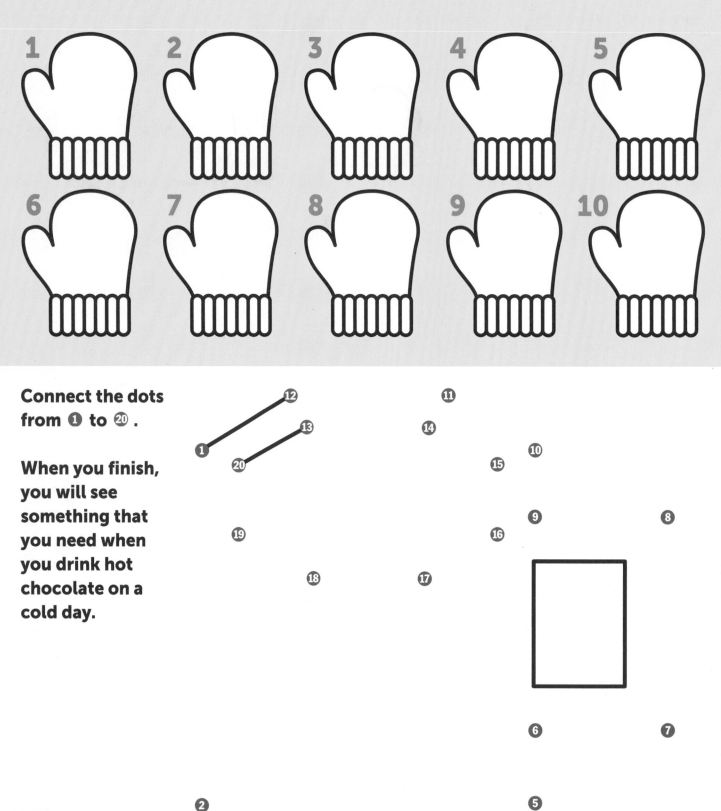

Connect the dots from ① to ⑳.

When you finish, you will see something that you need when you drink hot chocolate on a cold day.

Art by Mary Sullivan

83

Trim the Tree

There are **12** differences between these pictures. How many can you find?

Art by Bridget Starr Taylor

85

Hidden Pictures
Christmas Cactus

Can you find the **15** objects hidden in the big picture?

artist's brush

handbag

fishhook

slice of cake

pennant

banana

domino

button

86

Art by Neil Numberman

open book

ladle

boot

mitten

lollipop

hammer

glove

Snow Code

Using this snowflake alphabet, see if you can figure out what the skaters are saying.

Whirling Weather Words

A gust of wind separated some 8-letter weather words into pairs of letters. Rearrange the letter pairs after each definition to figure out the words.

Example: rays of brightness from our nearest star

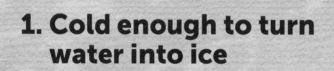 = sunlight

1. Cold enough to turn water into ice

2. Cloud cover with no sun visible

st er ov ca

3. Prediction of upcoming weather

re ca fo st

4. Measurement of water-drop precipitation

in ll fa ra

5. Moisture in the air di mi ty hu

6. Severe snowstorm rd iz za bl

7. Very light rain shower ri nk sp le

8. Weather warning ry ad so vi

Puzzle by Sherry Timberman; Art by J. Moffatt and B. Hoffman

Frosty and Friends

Each snowman has one that looks exactly like it. Can you find all the matching pairs?

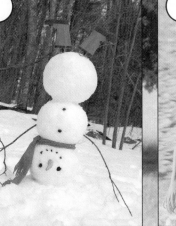

91

Hidden Pictures
Cocoa Break

Can you find the **12** objects hidden in the big picture?

ruler

gingerbread
cookie

sled

lollipop

arrow

bell

candy
cane

cloud

pennant

drinking
straw

mushroom

broom

Snow

A Story without Words

Make an Advent Wreath

By Susan Shadle Erb

For families that observe Advent, this simple wreath can make family time "brighter"!

1. Glue **colored paper** around four short **cardboard tubes**.
2. Glue **white paper** around a fifth tube.
3. Cut flames from **tissue paper**.
4. Cut pine branches from colored paper. Glue them onto a large **cardboard circle** or a **heavy-duty paper plate**.
5. Tape or glue the candles onto the wreath.
6. Decorate the wreath with real **pinecones**.
7. Each Sunday of Advent, "light" a candle by pushing a tissue-paper flame inside the tube. Add a flame to the white candle on Christmas Eve or Christmas Day.

What's an Advent Wreath?

For many Christians, Advent is the season of waiting for the Messiah. The word Advent means "arrival" or "coming." Advent begins four Sundays before Christmas Day and leads up to Christmas. As part of the observance, families or churches may light candles on an Advent wreath.

The four candles around the wreath often represent principles such as hope, love, peace, and joy. During a service or a family celebration, one candle is lit on the first Sunday of Advent, two candles on the second Sunday, and so on.

The colors of these candles vary among different churches and faiths. Many use three purple candles and one rose-colored candle, while others use four blue, purple, or white candles or other symbolic colors.

Some people place a white candle in the center of the wreath to represent Jesus, who Christians believe is the Messiah, and his birth, which many Christians celebrate on Christmas. This white candle is lit on Christmas Eve or Christmas Day, along with the other four candles.

Hidden Pictures Snow-friend

Can you find the **13** objects hidden in the big picture?

Art by Catherine Copeland

ruler

beehive

snail

eyeglasses

mallet

castle

comb

ax

drumstick

snake

heart

fried egg

coin

Crisscross Snowman

Fill in the snowman puzzle with words from the WORD LIST below. Use the number of letters in each word as a clue to where it might fit. We filled in 1 word to get you started.

WORD LIST

3 LETTERS
HAT

4 LETTERS
~~COAT~~
COLD
SLED

5 LETTERS
SCARF

6 LETTERS
FROZEN
ICICLE
SHOVEL
WINTER

7 LETTERS
MITTENS
SNOWMAN

8 LETTERS
~~BLIZZARD~~
EARMUFFS
SNOWBALL

9 LETTERS
~~SNOWFLAKE~~

Hidden Pictures
Santa's Band

Can you find the 15 objects hidden in the big picture?

screwdriver

crown

sock

pencil

sailboat

golf club

seashell

flowerpot

Art by David Helton

necktie

loaf of bread

chili pepper

wedge of lemon

leaf

puzzle piece

kite

A Slippery Slope

Grab a snowboard or sled, and slide through the **10** words that connect SCARF to BOOTS. Read the first clue and fill in the word. Then check the snowboard tracks to see which letters slide down to the next word. Have a good run!

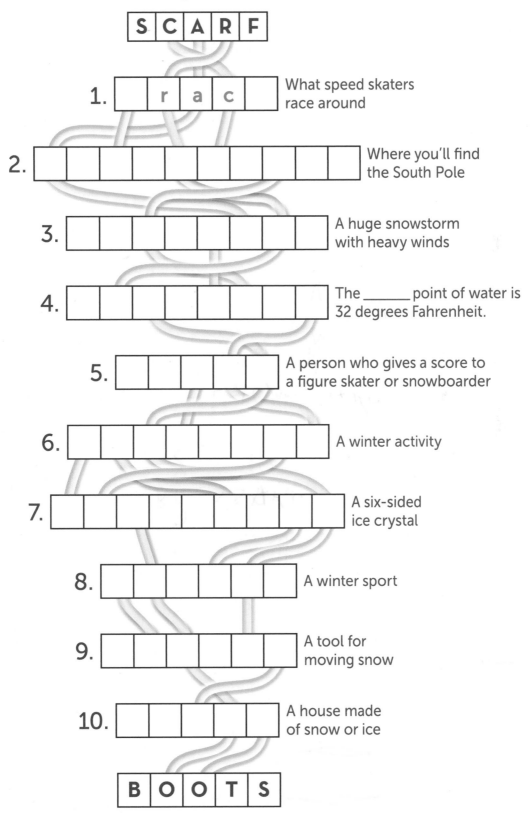

S | C | A | R | F

1. | | r | a | c | | What speed skaters race around

2. Where you'll find the South Pole

3. A huge snowstorm with heavy winds

4. The _____ point of water is 32 degrees Fahrenheit.

5. A person who gives a score to a figure skater or snowboarder

6. A winter activity

7. A six-sided ice crystal

8. A winter sport

9. A tool for moving snow

10. A house made of snow or ice

B | O | O | T | S

Puzzle by Andrew Brisman; Photo © Corbis/SuperStock

Angel Greetings

Follow the directions to cross out certain boxes. When you're done, write the remaining letters in order from left to right and top to bottom. They will give you the answer to the riddle.

Cross out all numbers divisible by 3.
Cross out all numbers divisible by 4.

S 6 ✗	H 14	M 16	T 21	A 28	D 64
N 33	R 9	E 39	A 22	P 42	B 56
F 44	L 31	J 3	Q 4	U 20	O 38
G 57	W 40	T 25	Y 45	I 18	X 32
H 50	Z 15	K 27	E 47	C 39	A 54
M 51	R 19	V 30	P 52	D 8	E 26

What do angels say when they run into a friend?

__ __ __ __, __ __ __ __ __ !

Peak Performance

Cleo planted a flag at the top of Mount Mammoth. It's your job to place a number on that flag. Start at the bottom. Add the numbers on 2 flags and place the sum in the flag above them. Keep going till you reach the top.

71

27   44   31   19

Art by Barbara Gray

Every sweater in the picture has another one that looks just like it. Find all **10** matching pairs.

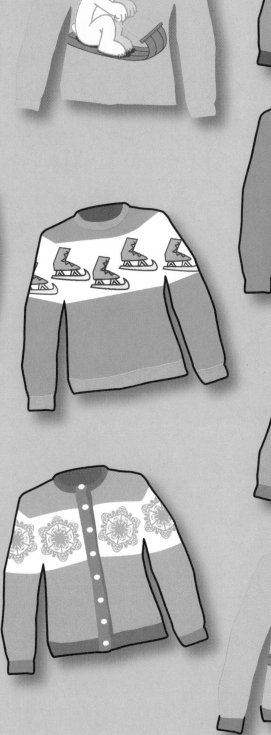

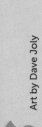

What's Wrong?

How many silly things can you find in this picture?

Art by David Helton

Plow a Path

The Hardwood County Commissioners need to conserve gas for their snowplow. Can you find a path that covers each road exactly once? The plow is parked in Maple City, so the route you choose should start and end there.

Lumber Rest

Oakville

Wooddale

Maple City

Walnut Crossing

Ashton

Twin Branch

Cherry Grove

Art by Holly Kowit

Hidden Pictures
Superchallenge!

There are 30 objects hidden in this scene. Without clues or knowing what to look for, try to find them all. Good luck!

106

Ornaments
ALL YOUR OWN

Add some personal touches to your Christmas tree. You can also hang any of these homemade decorations in a window or tie one to a present.

Cookie-Cutter Star

1. Tie one end of a piece of thin ribbon to a **small bell**. Tie the other end to a **star cookie cutter** so the small bell hangs in the center.

2. Glue more ribbon to the outside of the cookie cutter, making a loop at the top for a hanger. Let dry.

Mexican Tin Art

1. Use **permanent markers** to draw and decorate an animal shape or other design on the bottom of a disposable **aluminum pie tin**.

2. Cut out the shape.

3. Punch a hole through the shape. Tie **yarn** through the hole to hang.

Fabric-Patch Ball

1. Cut out small pieces of **fabric**. Place one piece on a **3-inch plastic-foam ball**. Gently press the corners of the fabric into the ball with a butter knife.

2. Overlap a second piece of fabric along one edge of the first piece of fabric, and press in. Continue until the entire ball is covered.

3. Make a loop with some **ribbon**, and pin it to the patched ball to hang.

Tree-mendous

How many silly things can you find in this picture?

Art by Bill Basso

Snow Code

Using the snowflake alphabet below, see
if you can figure out this funny poem.

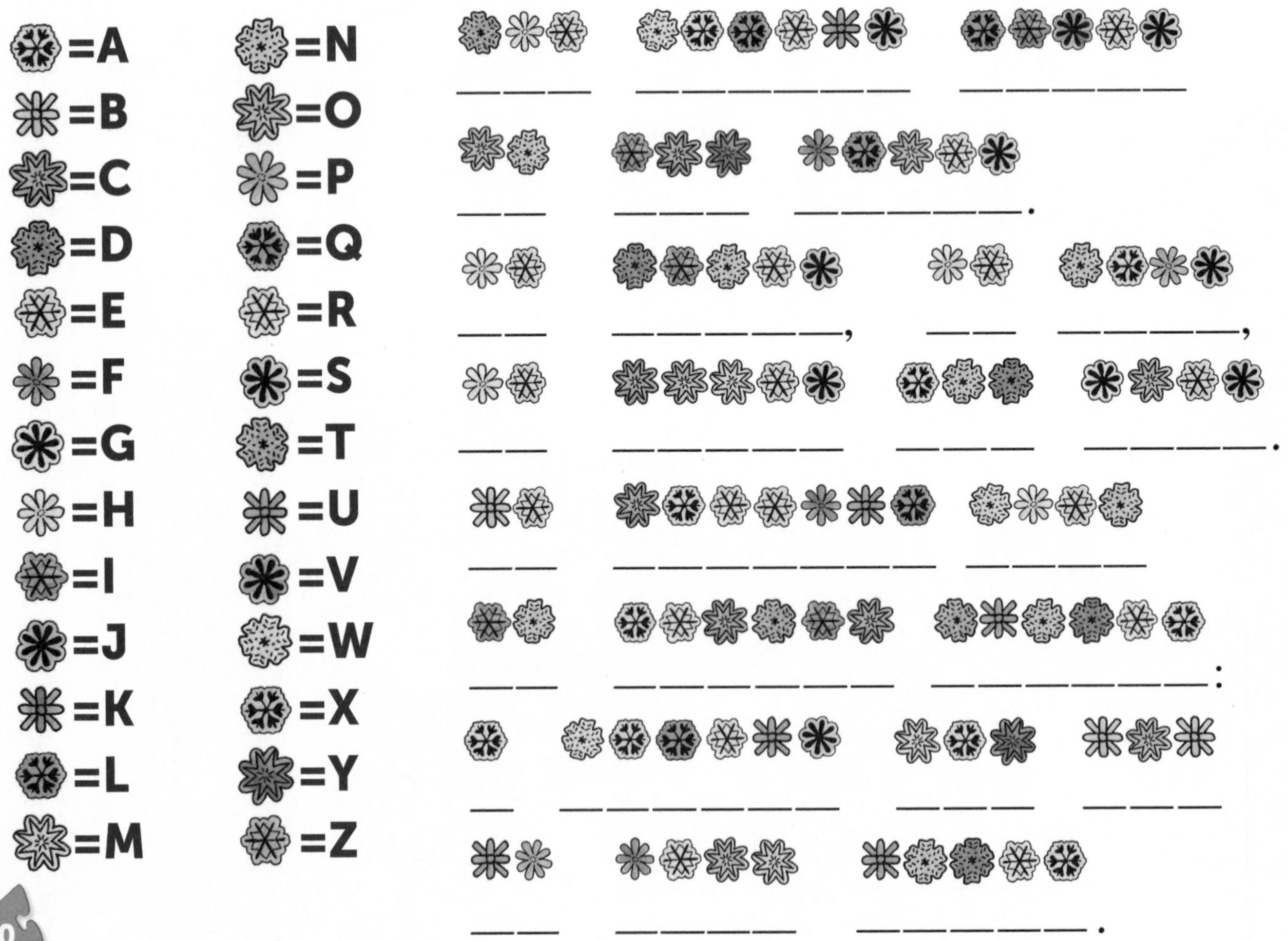

=A　　=N
=B　　=O
=C　　=P
=D　　=Q
=E　　=R
=F　　=S
=G　　=T
=H　　=U
=I　　=V
=J　　=W
=K　　=X
=L　　=Y
=M　　=Z

Oh, Christmas Tree!

Can you help Liam and Charlotte decorate their Christmas tree?
Will it have tinsel and sparkling lights? Round, red ornaments? You decide!

Art by Gillian Flint

Hidden Pictures
Caroling Along

Can you find the 8 objects hidden in the big picture?

ruler

stamp

pencil

book

heart

comb

spool of thread

whale

Art by Dana Regan

Snow Way!

Simon and 3 of his friends shoveled snow for money. Each used some of his or her earnings to buy something. From the clues below, can you tell what each friend bought and how much it cost?

Use the chart to keep track of your answers. Put an **X** in each box that can't be true and an **O** in boxes that match.

	Video Game	Sweater	Art Supplies	Basketball	$50	$35	$30	$25
Simon								
Nora								
Oscar								
Wanda								

1. Nora's art supplies cost more than Oscar's item, but less than Wanda's.
2. Simon bought the only piece of clothing.
3. Wanda's item cost twice as much as Oscar's.
4. The sweater cost more than the art supplies, but the video game cost more than the sweater.

Double Boarding

There are **16** differences between these pictures. How many can you find?

Hidden Pictures
Gingerbread House

Can you find the **15** objects hidden in the big picture?

Art by R. Michael Palan

toothbrush

ring

teacup

candle

fishhook

tack

pencil

golf club

needle

spatula

nail

wishbone

spoon

snake

handbell

Hat's Off

This snowman's head is getting cold.
Can you help him reach his hat?

Art by Charles Jordan

Which Candy?

Which candy was **NOT USED** on the gingerbread house?
Which candy **WAS USED** but isn't shown here?

Art by Helena Bogosian

Christmas Cutouts

These light and festive ornaments will brighten your holidays.

You Will Need:

- PLASTIC-FOAM TRAYS
- PERMANENT MARKERS
- GLITTER
- HOLE PUNCH
- RIBBON
- SEWING NEEDLE
- METALLIC THREAD

1. Draw your favorite holiday shape on a plastic-foam tray. Cut it out.

2. Decorate with markers, glitter, and whatever else you'd like to use.

3. Punch a hole in the top of the ornament.

4. Thread a piece of satin ribbon through the hole. Or with a sewing needle, attach metallic thread to the ornament. Knot the ends.

More Ideas

Get creative with your shapes and designs. Stars, candy canes, and angels are only a few of the possibilities. Love cartoons? Have a cartoon-character Christmas with plastic foam, glue, and magazine cutouts.

Photos by Hank Schneider

Spread the Joy!

Can you feel the holiday joy in the air? Find **JOY** and **19** other festive words in the grid below by looking up, down, backward, and diagonally.

```
S  H  F  C  A  N  D  L  E  S  A
D  U  V  E  O  A  H  R  A  D  S
N  P  P  Y  C  H  Y  E  S  R  T
E  Y  L  L  O  J  L  E  H  A  F
I  O  S  L  C  I  I  H  A  C  I
R  D  A  N  T  K  M  C  R  Y  G
F  S  G  N  O  S  A  L  E  S  Y
Y  O  J  O  H  W  F  E  O  Z  A
V  A  C  A  T  I  O  N  O  V  S
O  N  E  T  A  R  O  C  E  D  E
G  A  T  H  E  R  E  T  N  I  W
```

Word List

CANDLES	GIFTS
CARDS	HOT COCOA
CHEER	JOLLY
COOKIES	JOY
COZY	LOVE
DECORATE	SHARE
FAMILY	SNOW
FRIENDS	SONGS
FUN	VACATION
GATHER	WINTER

Have you circled all the words? Now write the leftover letters in order from left to right and top to bottom to spell out a message to you from Highlights.

____ _ _____ _____ _____!

Precise Ice

Hillary is getting ready for another competition. She's been practicing on this design all day. Can you show her how to make the design without crossing or retracing any lines?

Illustrated by Barbara Gray

Hidden Pictures
Christmas Train

Can you find the **13** objects hidden in the big picture?

sock

handbell

scissors

book

horn

pencil

sailboat

crown

toothbrush

football

saw

ring

ice-cream cone

Illustrated by Tim Davis

Shovel Trouble

Each of these shovelers left home without something. Use the visual clues to figure out what they need. Then find 4 clear paths in the snow that will lead each shoveler to the correct house.

Illustrated by Bill Basso

123

On the Twelfth Day of Christmas

The "gifts" just keep piling up! Can you count down the 37 here?

- 3 flying birds
- 3 pencils
- 3 slices of cake
- 2 books
- 2 shoes
- 2 socks
- balloon
- banana
- baseball cap
- butterfly
- chair
- chick
- dolphin
- domino
- duck
- flamingo
- gingerbread cookie
- goose
- ice-cream cone
- lamp
- pear
- penguin
- pitcher
- half an apple
- slice of pie
- star
- thermometer
- violin case

Also spy the:

- letter A
- numeral 3

Look, too, for the heads of:

- 4 birds
- 2 ducks
- 2 rabbits
- 1 boy
- 1 dog
- 1 fox

Art by Jerome Weisman

What's Wrong?

How many silly things can you find in this picture?

Illustrated by Kelly Kennedy

Sledding Hill

After a snowfall, everyone gathers to have fun on the big hill.

Can you find these items in the picture on the next page? Be sure to find the right number of each.

Use your crayons to finish and decorate this snowman.

1 snow shovel

2 red sleds

3 animals

4 blue boots

5 scarves

6 pine trees

126

Illustrated by Monica Wellington

127

Every winter hat in the picture has another one that looks just like it. Find all **10** matching pairs.

Illustrated by Dave Joly

Hidden Pictures Warming Up

Can you find the **14** objects hidden in the big picture?

Illustrated by Iryna Bodnaruk

plunger

pennant

ice-cream cone

feather duster

crown

boomerang

open book

rolling pin

mallet

tennis ball

dustpan

horseshoe

pencil

butter knife

Crisscross Mug

Fill in the mug puzzle with words from the WORD LIST below. Use the number of letters in each word as a clue to where it might fit. We filled in 1 word to get you started.

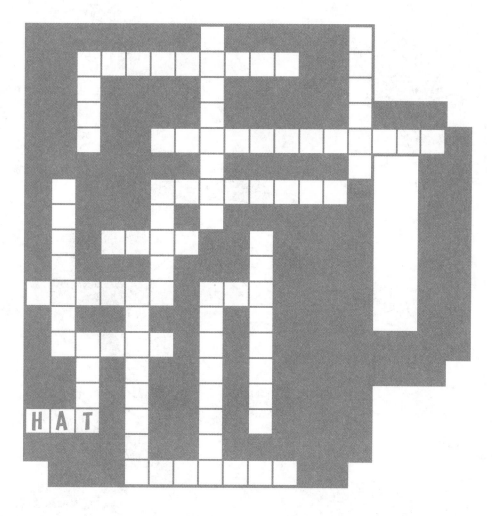

H A T

Word List

3 LETTERS
~~HAT~~
SKI

4 LETTERS
COAT
SLED
SNOW

5 LETTERS
BOOTS
SCARF

6 LETTERS
GLOVES
ICICLE

7 LETTERS
GOGGLES
SKI LIFT

8 LETTERS
BLIZZARD
EARMUFFS
MOUNTAIN
SKI LODGE
SNOWBALL

9 LETTERS
SNOWBOARD

12 LETTERS
HOT CHOCOLATE

Hidden Pictures
Skiing with Santa

Can you find the **12** objects hidden in the big picture?

mushroom

hockey stick

envelope

doughnut

comb

ice-cream bar

cactus

flyswatter

heart

banana

artist's brush

pie

Illustrated by Peter Grosshauser

Answers

5 Holiday Wrap-Up

6–7 Making Cookies

8 Reindeer Games

1–D/B   2–R   3–C/C   4–D/D   5–P/V

12 Cookie Code

1. MACAROON
2. LEMON BAR
3. SUGAR
4. FORTUNE
5. GINGERSNAP
6. SHORTBREAD
7. OATMEAL RAISIN
8. PEANUT BUTTER
9. CHOCOLATE CHIP
10. SNICKERDOODLE

What did the gingerbread man use to trim his fingernails?

A COOKIE CUTTER

10 Follow the Flakes

Here's one solution. You may have found others.

13 A New Friend

14 Downhill Run

133

Answers

15 Welcome to the North Pole

16–17 Match Maker

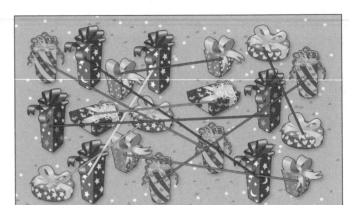

22–23 A Puzzling Present

20–21 Break the Ice

YOU WOULD HAVE TEN INCHES OF SNOW.

24 Scrambled Scarves

1. Katie
2. Grace
3. David
4. Matt

25 Precise Ice

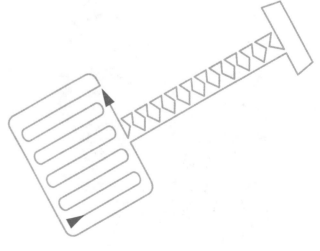

26 Knit Pick

27 Good Enough to Eat!

28 Double Snowmen

29 Santa's Coming to Town

Mike: Basketball   Christy: Video Game

Dave: Books   Neal: Skateboard

                       Jessica: Puzzle

30–31 Match-Up: *BRRRR!*

Pair: 1 and 7   Pair: 5 and 18   Pair: 10 and 15

Pair: 2 and 24   Pair: 6 and 19   Pair: 12 and 17

Pair: 3 and 23   Pair: 8 and 21   Pair: 13 and 16

Pair: 4 and 11   Pair: 9 and 22   Pair: 14 and 20

                  Single: 25

34 Winter Find

```
S N O W F L A K E I
N G M I T T E N S C
O B O O T S J Q N I
W L V S K I S X Y C
S I Y N J V C Y N L
H Z C O C O A S B E
O Z G W P A R K A S
E A J M Q V F A L L
Q R V A I C E T L E
Y D G N S L E E T D
```

36–37 The Perfect Tree

135

Answers

38 Christmas Crossword

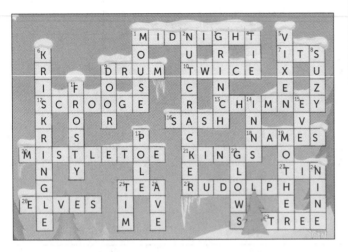

39 Wrapping Up

Amber: Green Gift, Blue Bow
Billy: Blue Gift, Yellow Bow
Chad: Red Gift, Green Bow
Daphne: Yellow Gift, Red Bow

40 Precise Ice

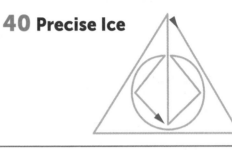

42 Tic Tac Row

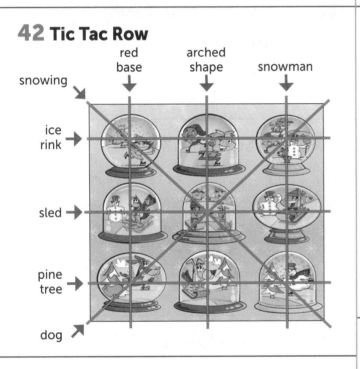

43 Santa's Day Off

46 Christmas-Tree Farm

THEY ALWAYS DROP THEIR NEEDLES.

47 Snowshoe Globes

44–45 Let It Snow

136

Answers

48—49 Double Skis

54 Snow Code

DID ANYONE LAUGH WHEN YOU FELL?

NO, BUT THE ICE MADE A FEW CRACKS!

52 Winter Word Mash

SNOWSHOES

SNOW GLOBE

SNOWCONE

SNOWMAN

SNOWMOBILE

52—53 Go for a Spin

1. SLEDDING
8. GLOVES
13. SNOWFLAKE
21. ELVES
25. SCARF
29. FREEZES
35. SLUSH
39. HOT COCOA
46. ANTARCTICA
55. ARCTIC
60. COAT
63. TEETH
67. HEATS
71. SNOWMAN
77. NUMB
80. BLOW
83. WINTER
88. RINK
91. KNITS
95. SPRING

55 Christmas in the City

56 Warm Homecoming

57 Festive Word Hunt

58 Santa's Workshop

137

Answers

59 Tricky Trees

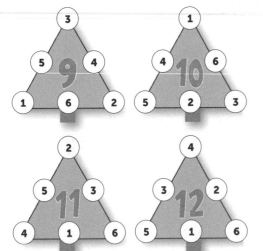

60–61 Flake Search

62 Winter Word Hunt

63 Christmas Party Fun

64 Snow Angels

Stefanie
Scarf #1

Sabrina
Scarf #2

Sara
Scarf #3

Sue
Scarf #4

65 Snowflake Path

YOU DID IT

Answers

68–69 Winter Wonder

70 Mele Kalikimaka!

71 Snowman Match

72–73 Let's Skate!

Here's one solution.
You may have found others.

74 Precise Ice

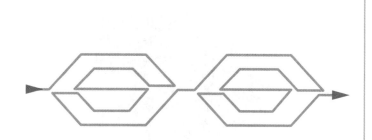

75 That's a Wrap!

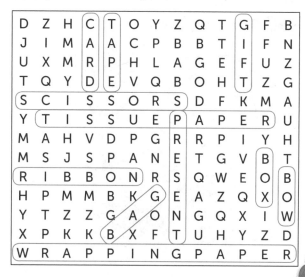

139

Answers

76–77 House Sweet House

78–79 The Cold and the Beautiful

80 Snow Go

82–83 Mitten Search

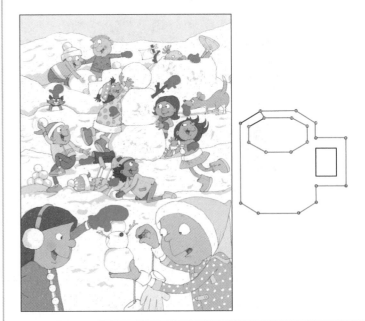

84–85 Trim the Tree

86 Christmas Cactus

Answers

87 Snow Code

WHAT DO SNOWMEN
LIKE TO RIDE?

ICE-CYCLES!

88–89 Whirling Weather Words

1. freezing
2. overcast
3. forecast
4. rainfall
5. humidity
6. blizzard
7. sprinkle
8. advisory

90–91 Frosty and Friends

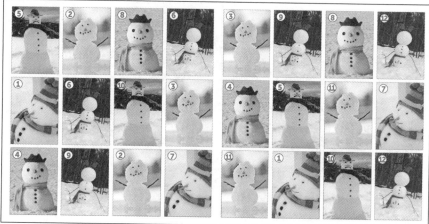

92–93 Cocoa Break

98 Santa's Band

96 Snow-friend

97 Crisscross Snowman

99 A Slippery Slope

SCARF
1. TRACK
2. ANTARCTICA
3. BLIZZARD
4. FREEZING
5. JUDGE
6. SLEDDING
7. SNOWFLAKE
8. HOCKEY
9. SHOVEL
10. IGLOO
BOOTS

100 Angel Greetings

HALO, THERE!

141

Answers

101 Peak Performance

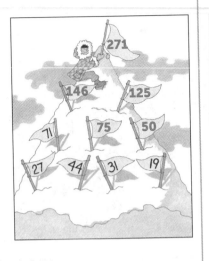

102-103 Match Maker

105 Plow a Path

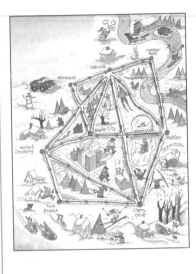

106–107 Superchallenge!

110 Snow Code

THE WALRUS LIVES
ON ICY FLOES.
HE DINES, HE NAPS,
HE COMES AND GOES.
BE CAREFUL WHEN
IN ARCTIC TUNDRA:
A WALRUS MAY BOB
UP FROM UNDRA.

112 Caroling Along

113 Snow Way!

Simon: Sweater, $35
Nora: Art Supplies, $30
Oscar: Basketball, $25
Wanda: Video Game, $50

114 Double Boarding

115 Gingerbread House

116 Hat's Off

117 Which Candy?

120 Spread the Joy!

HAVE A HAPPY HOLIDAY SEASON!

121 Precise Ice

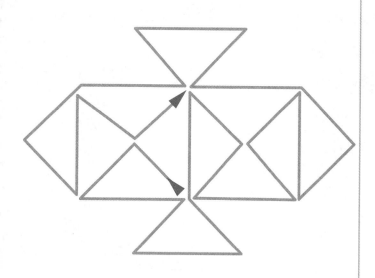

122 Christmas Train

Answers

123 Shovel Trouble

124 On the Twelfth Day of Christmas

126–127 Sledding Hill

128–129 Match Maker

130 Warming Up

131 Crisscross Mug

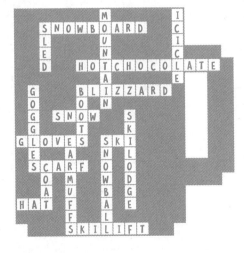

132 Skiing with Santa